FORGIVENESS

LIVING
THE GOOD LIFE
TOGETHER

FORGIVENESS
letting go

study & reflection guide

Susan Pendleton Jones
and L. Gregory Jones

ABINGDON PRESS / Nashville

LIVING THE GOOD LIFE TOGETHER
FORGIVENESS: LETTING GO
Study & Reflection Guide

Copyright © 2006 by Abingdon Press

This book is printed on acid-free, elemental chlorine-free paper.

ISBN 0-687-46610-5

06 07 08 09 10 11 12 13 14 15—10 9 8 7 6 5 4 3 2 1
MANUFACTURED IN THE UNITED STATES OF AMERICA

Contents

—1—

An Introduction to This Study Series

PSALM FOR PRAYING

Psalm 103:8, 11-12

The LORD is merciful and gracious,
   slow to anger and abounding in steadfast love.
....
For as the heavens are high above the earth,
   so great is his steadfast love toward those who
      fear him;
as far as the east is from the west,
   so far he removes our transgressions from us.

CHRISTIAN CHARACTER IN COMMUNITY

THE GREAT EARLY Christian theologian Augustine opens his *Confessions* with these famous words: "Restless is our heart until it comes to rest in thee." Augustine, who had himself led a life of distorted and disordered desires that left him frustrated and without satisfaction, eventually discovered that we only find satisfaction when we rest in God. We are created for life with God, and only through God's love will we discover the rest, wholeness, and fullness we most truly desire.

So how can we discover this fullness of life that we yearn for, especially when we try and try but can't seem to get any satisfaction? Ironically, we will only discover it when we quit trying so hard. Instead, we need to learn to rest in God, the God who loves us and embraces us before we can do anything. God's grace invites us to discover that we cannot earn love; we can only discover it in the gift of being loved.

So far, so good. But it seems easier said than done. After all, to receive the gift of being loved calls for us to love in return. And yet we lack the skills—and often the desire—to love in the way God loves us. As a result, as wonderful as it sounds to "rest in God," to discover "the gift of being loved by God," we fear that we are not up to the relationship.

In order to truly receive love, we want to become like the lover. So for us to truly receive God's love, we are called to become like God—and that sounds both inviting and scary. Become like God? This becomes even more daunting when we discover that this gracious, loving God is also the one who is called "holy" and calls us through God's love to be holy as well. Jesus even enjoins us to be "perfect" as our "heavenly Father is perfect" (Matthew 5:48). The task begins to seem overwhelming. How does this relate to the idea of resting in God's grace?

The wonder and joy of Christian life is that we are invited by God into a way of life, a life of abundance in which we learn to cultivate habits of desiring, thinking, feeling, and living that continually open us to the grace of God's holiness. The invitation to Christian life is an invitation to discover that "the good life" is lived in the light of God's grace. When we embark on a truly Christian life, we learn to become holy not by trying really hard but by continually being drawn into the disciplined habits of living as friends of God in the community of others.

This may seem odd at first, but think about it in terms of learning to play the piano. We're drawn by the desire to play beautiful music. But before we can play beautiful music, we have to learn basic habits: the position of our hands, the scales of the piano, the role of the foot pedals, and the rhythms of music. Over time, as we learn these basic skills, our teachers invite us to take on more challenging tasks. Eventually, we find ourselves playing with both hands, learning to master more complicated arrangements of music, and perhaps even integrating the foot pedals into our playing. If we practice the piano long enough, we will reach a point where it seems effortless to play—and even to improvise new music—in the company of others.

It's around this metaphor of practice that Living the Good Life Together: A Study of Christian Character in Community has been developed. Rather than to practice being piano players, this series of small-group studies is aimed at helping persons practice being Christian. Each unit of study is designed to move persons from *understanding* various aspects of Christian character to the development of *practices* reflective of those aspects of Christian character to, ultimately, the *embodiment* of Christian character in community. In other words, the idea is to educate the desires of heart and mind in order to develop, over time, patterns of living like Christ.

A billboard or bumper sticker would say it more succinctly: "The Good Life: Get It. Try It. Live It—Together."

Living the Good Life Together gets at the heart of the life God intends for us, particularly as it relates to others in community. Attentiveness, forgiveness, discernment, intimacy, humility, hospitality—these are some of the aspects of the life God intends for us. And they are the subjects of this study series.

STUDY FORMAT

The overall process of this study series is based on some of Jesus' own words to his followers: "Come and see" (John 1:39) and "Go and do likewise" (Luke 10:37). In each study, the first six sessions are the backbone of the "Come and See" portion. These sessions inspire and teach the group about a particular character trait of the Christian life. The second six sessions are the "Go and Do" portion. For these sessions, the study offers tools to help group members plan how to put into practice what they have learned.

"Come and See"

Session 1: An Introduction to This Study Series

This session is an orientation to the twelve-week study. It provides information about the Living the Good Life Together series and an introduction to the trait of Christian character addressed in that particular study.

Sessions 2–5: Topics in Christian Character

These sessions offer information about aspects of the particular trait of Christian character. The sessions will help group members explore the trait and will foster intimacy with Scripture, with others, and with God.

Session 6: Planning the Next Steps Together

In this session, group members plan what they will do together in Sessions 7–12 to practice the Christian character trait they have learned about in the previous sessions.

"Go and Do"

Sessions 7–12: From Study to Practice

In these sessions, group members will carry out their plans from Session 6, putting their learnings into practice.

USING THE RESOURCE COMPONENTS

The resource components of Living the Good Life Together—the study & reflection guide, leader guide, and DVD—and the group sessions function together to foster intimacy with Scripture, with others, and with God. This takes place through a broad range of approaches: reading, writing, discussion, viewing video, prayer, worship, and practical application.

Study & Reflection Guide

This book serves as a guide for individual preparation from week to week, as a personal journal for responding to all elements of the study, and as a planning tool for the "Go and Do" portion of the study. Becoming familiar with the following content sections will enhance the effectiveness of this guide.

Psalm for Praying

A psalm text appears on the first page of each session of the study & reflection guide. It's there for you to use as a prayer of invocation as you begin your study each day.

Daily Readings

Reading these passages each day is central to your preparation for the group meeting. Consider reading from different translations of the Bible to hear familiar texts in a fresh way. Ask what the Scriptures mean in light of the session's theme and how they apply to your own life. Be alert to insights and questions you would like to remember for the group meeting, and jot those down in the boxes provided in this study & reflection guide.

Reflections

The space at the bottom of each page in each content session of the study & reflection guide is provided for making notes or recording any thoughts or questions the reading brings to mind.

Lectio Divina

Each session of this study will include a prayer exercise called *lectio divina*, sometimes called "praying the Scriptures." The practice of lectio divina, which is Latin for "sacred reading," continues to gain popularity as people discover anew this ancient and meaningful approach to prayer.

In the practice of lectio divina outlined below, we listen, as the Benedictines instruct, "with the ear of the heart" for a word, phrase, sound, or image that holds a special meaning for us. This could be a word of comfort, instruction, challenge, or assurance. It could be an image suggested by a word, and the image could take us to a place of deep reverence or personal introspection.

It's important to note that like the biblical exercises in this book, lectio divina is about what is evoked in you as you experience the text. Now is not the time for historical-critical musings or scholarly interpretations of the text. It's time for falling in love with the Word and experiencing the goodness of God.

Step One: *Silencio.* After everyone has turned to the Scripture, be still. Silently turn all your thoughts and desires over to God. Let go of concerns, worries, or agendas. Just *be* for a few minutes.

Step Two: *Lectio.* Read the short passage of Scripture slowly and carefully, either aloud or silently. Reread it. Be alert to any word, phrase, or image that invites you, that puzzles you, that intrigues you. Wait for this word, phrase, or image to come to you; try not to rush it.

Step Three: *Meditatio.* Take the word, phrase, or image from your Scripture passage that comes to you and ruminate over it. Repeat it to yourself. Allow this word, phrase, or image to engage your thoughts, your desires, your memories. You may share your word, phrase, or image with others in the group, but don't feel pressured to speak.

Step Four: *Oratio.* Pray that God transform you through the word, phrase, or image from Scripture. Consider how this word, phrase, or image connects with your life and how God is made known to you in it. This prayer may be either silent or spoken.

Step Five: *Contemplatio.* Rest silently in the presence of God. Move beyond words, phrases, or images. Again, just *be* for a few minutes. Close this time of lectio divina with "Amen."[1]

Faithful Friends

True friends in faith are those who can help us hear the voice of God in our lives more clearly. They act as our mentors, our guides. At times they weep with us, and at other times they laugh with us. At all times they keep watch over us in love and receive our watch-care in return. Having a faithful friend (or friends) and being a faithful friend are at the heart of what it means to live as a Christian in community for at least three reasons:

- Faithful friends can at times challenge the sins we have come to love.
- Faithful friends will affirm the gifts we are afraid to claim.
- Faithful friends help us dream the dreams we otherwise wouldn't have imagined.

During this study, each group member will be invited to join with one or two others to practice being a faithful friend over the course of the twelve weeks and hopefully beyond. While there are no "mystical" qualifications for being a faithful friend, what *is* required is the willingness to be open to possibilities of guiding another person or persons into a deeper and richer experience of Christian living. Like all aspects of the Christian life, this activity of being a faithful friend is a discipline, a practice.

A key decision faithful friends will make is how to stay in touch week after week. Some may choose to meet over lunch or coffee or take a walk. Others may choose to use e-mail or the telephone. Whatever the means, consider using the following questions to stimulate an ongoing conversation over the course of the study:

- How has it gone for you, trying to live the week's practice?
- What's been hard about it?
- What's been easy or comfortable?
- What challenges have there been? What rewards?
- What kinds of things happened this week—at work, at home, in your prayer life—that you want to talk about? Has anything affected your spiritual life and walk?

There's an old African proverb that says, "If you want to go fast, go alone. If you want to go far, go together." In the end, a faithful friend is someone who is willing to go the distance with you, following Christ all the way. The aim of this feature of the study is to move you further down the way of Christian discipleship in the company of another.

FORGIVENESS: LETTING GO

We've been introduced to the study series Living the Good Life Together. Now it's time to turn our attention to the particular trait of Christian character that we'll be exploring and focusing upon throughout this study: *forgiveness*.

Former presidents, great poets, Pulitzer Prize–winning authors and artists, scientists, religious leaders, and behavioral experts—all these have testified to the power and place of forgiveness in human life. Convicted felons, public school teachers, victims of war, and mothers raising children—these too know the power and place of forgiveness.

In our war-torn world as well as in the torn places of our own hearts, forgiveness offers a promise of reconciliation and hope. There are even groups that specifically dedicate themselves to forgiveness. For example, the Forgiveness Project is a national group that counters violence with the practice of forgiveness and conflict resolution. The John Templeton Foundation sponsors forgiveness studies to research the effects of forgiveness on the human body and on human relationships. South Africa, with its Truth and Reconciliation Commission, has become a laboratory of sorts for the efforts of religious leaders and government politicians to bring about forgiveness and healing.

Jesus' teachings on forgiveness are rich and varied. They're straightforward and direct, but they also bear close study, because some are not what they might seem at first glance. Jesus encouraged forgiveness when he taught about the prodigal son, when he encountered the woman at the well, and when he was confronted by those who were unforgiving and unkind.

These next five sessions in FORGIVENESS: LETTING GO rely upon the idea that forgiving and being forgiven are critical parts of our life in the faith. Session 2, "The Heart of Christian Living," places forgiveness in the center of our lives as Christians. Session 3, "Crafting Communities of Forgiveness," explores what it means to be a forgiving community. Session 4, "The Dance of Forgiveness," encourages us to practice forgiveness, step by step, in our everyday lives. Session 5, "Challenges to Forgiveness," invites us to persevere in the difficult journey of forgiveness. Session 6, "Planning the Next Steps Together," facilitates the group planning process for putting into practice what members have learned about forgiveness.

Forgiveness is basic to who we are as Christians and to how we live in the world. It's such a powerful force that Reinhold Niebuhr called it "the final possibility of love in history."[2] Because of that—and because forgiveness can sometimes be elusive or misunderstood—the study of forgiveness is an important part of our efforts to live the good life together.

—2—

The Heart of Christian Living

Psalm 139:23-24

Search me, O God, and know my heart;
   test me and know my thoughts.
See if there is any wicked way in me,
   and lead me in the way everlasting.

Daily Readings

DAY ONE
2 Corinthians 5:16-20 *(The ministry of reconciliation)*

DAY TWO
1 John 4:13-19 *(God's perfect love for us)*

DAY THREE
Luke 15:1-32 *(The parables of the lost coin, lost sheep, and lost son)*

THE HEART OF CHRISTIAN LIVING

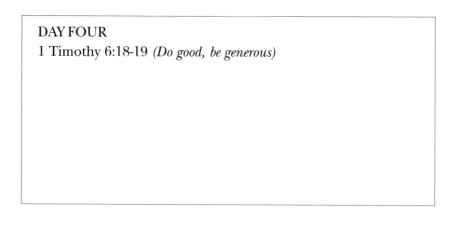

DAY FOUR
1 Timothy 6:18-19 *(Do good, be generous)*

DAY FIVE
Matthew 18:23-35 *(The parable of the unforgiving servant)*

DAY SIX
Read the chapter on pages 20–27. You may take notes in the space provided at the bottom of each page.

I N ONE OF THE CLASSIC *Peanuts* comic strips, Lucy is leaning on Schroeder's piano, looking adoringly at him. Yet
Schroeder, as usual, is ignoring her. So Lucy asks, "Schroeder,
do you know what love is?" In the next frame, Schroeder is standing, looking straight at the reader as he says, "Love. A noun. To
have affection for, to be devoted to." He then sits back down and
resumes playing the piano, still ignoring Lucy. She then looks out
at the reader with an exasperated look on her face and observes,
"On paper, he's great."[3]

Christians face such a predicament. We can be a lot like
Schroeder when it comes to forgiveness. On paper, we're great,
but how we actually live our lives is another matter. Too often
Christians as individuals and churches as communities seem to
mirror—or even intensify—the brokenness that's already found in
the world. Rather than offer a window
into the gracious character of God's
love, we continue the cycles of violence,
vengeance, and destructiveness that are
marks of sin.

**Forgiveness is a central theme of
the good life as outlined in
Scripture.**

Forgiveness is a central theme of
the good life as outlined in Scripture.
It's embodied in the person and work
of Christ. It's a focal point of the
Lord's Prayer and the Apostles' Creed. It's crucial to services of
baptism and Communion. And in most churches, it's an integral
theme in regular patterns of Sunday worship. But even with all
these reminders of how important forgiveness is, when we
attempt to apply it to our daily lives, we still fall short.

reflections

CHRISTIAN CHARACTER IN CONTEXT

Jesus' answer to the brokenness of people's lives was to embody God's forgiveness. By spending time with them and offering them dignity and new life, Jesus helped heal them. Some of them knew they were lost. Others feared they were, and they came to Jesus to ask him, "What must I do to inherit eternal life?" Others asked him, "Lord, will you make me clean?" and "Lord, teach us to pray." (See Luke 5:12; 10:25; 11:1; 18:18.)

But many of the people Jesus encountered didn't even realize they were lost. When Jesus ate with sinners, he angered the scribes and the Pharisees, who were the religious leaders of first-century Palestine. The stories he told showed that they were just as lost as the sinners they complained about; they just didn't know it. They were angry because Jesus both welcomed sinners and had the audacity to eat with them, by his actions offering God's forgiveness to them.

Eating together was a very intimate act in first-century Palestine. There was a strong tradition of hospitality among Semitic people then as it is now. When you shared table fellowship with someone, it was a sign of full acceptance of the other person: "I believe in you; I will stake my reputation on you." Eating together was a sign of welcome, of embrace, even a sign of forgiveness. And Jesus did this with sinners and with tax collectors, with prostitutes and with other outcasts. He was offering them God's forgiveness—a place at God's table. The Hebrew Scriptures warn about associating with the wicked, so the religious leaders of Jesus' day were flabbergasted by his actions.

To help the scribes and Pharisees understand why he behaved this way, Jesus shares with them three parables in Luke 15.

reflections

21

These stories tell us about the character of God and give us a brief glimpse into the heart and mind of the one Jesus called "Father."

The first story is about a lost animal, the second about a lost object, and the third about two brothers and a forgiving father. "Which one of you, having a hundred sheep and losing one of them, does not leave the ninety-nine in the wilderness and go after the one that is lost until he finds it?" (15:4). "Or what woman having ten silver coins, if she loses one of them, does not light a lamp, sweep the house, and search carefully until she finds it?" (15:8). Who would do that? It doesn't make sense to us, but God says, "Let's do it. Let's go out after the one who is lost—even if it means risking the ninety-nine sheep just to regain one, or even if it takes extra time and effort to look endlessly for one lost coin. We cannot rejoice until all have been found."

Jesus tells the Pharisees that when one sinner repents, God rejoices so exuberantly, so freely that heaven itself joins in a song of praise. "Come, rejoice with me, for this one who was lost now is found. Let's have a party; let's slaughter the fatted calf. Let's have a feast and celebrate." That's what God says.

In the parable of the two brothers, we learn that the loving father not only welcomes the younger son—the one who is very much like those sinners and tax collectors—but he also invites the elder son—the one who seems an awful lot like those scribes and Pharisees—to join the party. The father wants both of his sons to feast and rejoice with him. God's love is wide and deep enough to embrace all—those who know they are lost and admit they need help *and* those who are too stubborn or too blind to see their own need. This is why God's grace is amazing, because it reaches out to all of us, no matter how sinful, prideful, stubborn, or blind we are.

reflections

What Should Our Theme Be?

When we began commissioning artwork for a new building at
Duke University Divinity School, one sculptor we spoke with
noticed in Greg's office a framed copy of Rembrandt's *The Return
of the Prodigal Son.* "That story should be our theme," she said.
So we sat with her and read Luke 15 over and over, asking how this
story could be portrayed in sculpture. We came to understand that
the story is incomplete without reference to both of the ungrateful
sons. Then we realized that it's the father who ties the story
together. So, we felt the end result should portray all three figures.
In the final sculpture, the frail, crookbacked father is in the center,
with his right arm around the younger son. The younger son peni-
tently kneels beside him with his left arm around the father's back,
his left hand resting on his father's heart. The elder son stands tall
on the other side of the father, his arms folded across his own
chest, leaning back, looking away. But the father's left hand is
reaching out to the elder son, trying to draw him in, and the
father is looking at him with a pleading, hopeful look.[4]

And there you have it—the "is" and the "ought." Reconciliation
is achieved but with much work left to be done. There's still the
aching, still the lingering consequences of sin. The elderly father
is frail and weary-worn. The younger son has empty pockets,
a bruised ego, and the knowledge that he has deeply hurt his
father. And yet amidst this brokenness, there's the vision of what
can be, as the father continues to reach out to the elder son, to
draw him in. In the words of Nicholas Wolterstorff, we're called
to live as "aching visionaries"[5]—those who yearn for God's kingdom to come in its fullness.

reflections

FEASTING ON FORGIVENESS

God's embrace is deep and wide. It expands outward, drawing all to the feast, calling all to celebrate, making a place for everyone at God's table. God invites us into the party to "feast on forgiveness," but too often we stand apart—like that elder brother—and refuse to come inside. We allow our world to contract. We focus inward on ourselves, on petty slights, hurt feelings, thoughtless oversights. It's much more tempting to be angry and resentful, to feel unappreciated, to pout and say, "It's just not fair."

Feasting on forgiveness—rather than on bitterness, anger, or revenge—allows us the freedom to live into a future not bound by the brokenness of the past. It gives us hope. Forgiveness is both receptive and active; it's something done *to* us and something done *by* us. We're called to forgive others, which can be very difficult. But we're also called to be forgiven for the wrongs we've done, an act that takes us out of control and places us at the mercy of the one whose forgiveness we seek. To embody forgiveness fully, we must *forgive* as well as *be forgiven*.

> **Feasting on forgiveness allows us the freedom to live into a future not bound by the brokenness of the past.**

Yet the very difficult issues of forgiveness remain. How can we receive forgiveness from God that genuinely frees us from our sin? How do we forgive those who have wronged us? How do we hold others accountable for their sin? Where is God in this process of forgiving and being forgiven? Can we bear the truth that God forgives even those whom we don't want to forgive? These are hard questions

reflections

that go to the very heart of what it means to be human. Who among us hasn't struggled with promises broken, hurtful words spoken in anger, acts of betrayal, feelings of hopelessness? Indeed, we have much to learn about forgiveness.

We learn how to forgive from the God who first forgave us in Christ. Christ forgives without condition, but we can only receive that forgiveness if we're set free to forgive others. The parable of the unforgiving servant (Matthew 18:23-35) illustrates how unlikely it seems that those forgiven a great debt would not respond by forgiving others. And yet it happens because we fail to connect our experience of the power of God's forgiveness in Christ with the call to forgive others.

A wise friend of ours once said, "Our ability to experience joy is discovered in our capacity to forgive." Only when we come to the point where we can forgive others for the wrongs done to us can we experience joy in its fullest. Feasting on forgiveness renews in us a sense of joy. These parables are evidence that God's mercy—that the searching heart of God—is actively at work. It's this mercy, this amazing grace that gives us reason to rejoice, to feast on forgiveness.

TAKING THE PIECES AND GIVING THEM BACK AGAIN

Toward the close of her hauntingly beautiful novel *Beloved,* Toni Morrison recounts a conversation between two friends, Sixo and Sethe. Both had been slaves most of their lives. Sixo had met a woman a few years before whom he called the "Thirty-Mile Woman" because he had to walk thirty miles to see her and spend

reflections

25

time with her. He tells Sethe about what this woman has meant in his life—how she had met him in all his brokenness and, over time, had mended his life. "The pieces I am," he says, "she gather them and give them back to me in all the right order."[6] God is like that. God takes the broken places of our lives, gathers them up, blesses them, and then offers them back to us in all the right order so that we may live in the world as the body of Christ.

One of the most powerful passages of Scripture in the New Testament is found in 2 Corinthians 5:16-20. Here, Paul reminds us that "in Christ God was reconciling the world to himself." God has entrusted to us this message of reconciliation and has made us "ambassadors for Christ," making an appeal for reconciliation through us.

Christian forgiveness—and *forgiven-ness*—is a way of life that must be learned and relearned on our journey toward holiness in God's kingdom. It requires the ever-deepening and ever-widening sense of what friendship with God and God's creatures entails. God's Spirit is at work forgiving, healing, and recreating us in the likeness of Christ for life in God's kingdom. Indeed, God's Spirit is at work in the ways we learn to forgive and be forgiven, to heal and be healed, to recreate and to be recreated in our lives with others. In this light, it becomes apparent that Christian forgiveness is not only a word spoken or heard, a gesture offered or received, an emotion experienced or transformed; it's a way of life to be lived in faithful response to the gracious love of God at work in our world and in our lives.

In order to live this life faithfully, we need to participate in Christian practices that shape virtuous living. At the most basic level, this is a simple appeal to common sense. We know that the habits we develop and try to instill in our children make a differ-

reflections

ence. Habits are crucial for learning to play the piano, paint beautiful portraits, or become a soccer player. We know that "practice makes perfect." Doesn't it make sense that the same principle is true in our lives as Christians? Now let's turn to the practices of the faith as we explore forgiveness and what it means to live the good life together.

reflections

FAITHFUL FRIENDS: WATCHING OVER ONE ANOTHER IN LOVE

Use this space to record thoughts, reflections, insights, prayer concerns, or other matters that arise from your weekly conversations with faithful friends.

—3—

Crafting Communities of Forgiveness

Psalm 32:3-5

While I kept silence, my body wasted away
    through my groaning all day long.
For day and night your hand was heavy
      upon me;
    my strength was dried up as by the heat
    of summer.

Then I acknowledged my sin to you,
    and I did not hide my iniquity;
I said, "I will confess my transgressions
    to the LORD,"
    and you forgave the guilt of my sin.

DAILY READINGS

DAY ONE
James 5:13-16 *(Confess your sins to one another)*

DAY TWO
Galatians 5:19-24; 6:2 *(The works of the flesh, the fruit of the Spirit)*

DAY THREE
Matthew 18:21-22 *(Seventy-seven times)*

DAY FOUR
Matthew 5:1-12 *(Sermon on the Mount)*

DAY FIVE
Ephesians 5:1-14 *(Live in love as Christ loved us)*

DAY SIX
Read the chapter on pages 32–37. You may take notes in the space provided at the bottom of each page.

SEVERAL YEARS AGO, AS SUSAN was putting our younger son to bed, after she had turned off the lights and said prayers, she bent down over his bed to kiss him goodnight. As she did, he reached up and pulled her face toward his. He gave her seven kisses on her forehead—four down and three across. As he let her go, he looked her in the eye and said, "Mom, you are blessed."

"Ben, did you realize you kissed me in the shape of a cross?" she asked him.

"Yep," he answered. "I planned it that way."

Over the years, Ben had seen the sign of the cross made on other people's foreheads, as well as his own, with ashes during Lent and with water during services of baptismal renewal. Never before, however, had he seen the sign of the cross made on the forehead in kisses. From this little boy, often so full of mischief, Susan received an unexpected sign of grace from God.

By observing Christian practices during Lenten and baptismal services, Ben had received a gift from the church. He was learning to understand the deep connection between living a blessed life and having that life shaped by practices marked by the crucified and risen Christ.

CHRISTIAN CHARACTER IN CONTEXT

Christian practices are what Christian people do together over time in response to God's active presence in the world. As such, these practices are indispensable for our spiritual lives and for shaping our lives in God as holy people.

reflections

The Christian practice of forgiveness gives us a way to address and even to overcome our sins, whether in community or in our individual lives. Such sins include things we *do* to one another (violence, adultery, lying, racist comments or actions) and things we *fail to do* for one another (abandoning those who suffer, neglecting the physical or emotional needs of others, refusing to act justly or truthfully). In either case, we not only diminish others; we diminish ourselves.

When we teach our seminary class entitled "Forgiveness and Reconciliation in the Church," there's never a shortage of stories for the students' case studies: fights between pastors and laity, tales of sexual misconduct, broken promises, lies told. These are things that tear people and communities apart.

This pervasiveness of sin, inside and outside the church, has the strong force of habit that is difficult to unlearn. Indeed, the habit of sinfulness eventually takes on the force of necessity. As a result, we find it increasingly difficult not only to escape sinfulness but even to *desire* to escape it. Instead of turning outward with self-giving love toward others, we turn inward on ourselves.

Thus Christian practices, particularly those related to forgiveness, must be bound up with the support and challenge of friends—especially with the friend who is God. Friends shape our thinking, feeling, and living. They challenge us and call us to repent and be transformed, because we trust one another. Through our friends, God calls us to ongoing conversion, to practices of Christian living that inspire daily repentance as they foster holiness.

> **Christian practices must be bound up with the support and challenge of friends.**

reflections

CHRISTIAN DISCIPLESHIP

Let's take a moment to consider what specific habits and practices of Christian discipleship should shape communities of Christians. Which practices in our lives together could inspire us for holy living? What could enable forgiveness to be passed on in powerful ways?

First and foremost, we need the practice of regularly wrestling with Scripture, not as isolated individuals but as a people shaped by a community's practices of reading. The aim of such practice is to make the language of God as familiar to us as our native tongue and to make the stories of God and God's people a vital part of our lives. This doesn't mean that wrestling with Scripture is necessarily easy or that we'll understand or like what we read. But too often today Christians don't even know the basic Scripture texts. There are significant numbers of people who profess their belief in the God of Jesus Christ yet are unable to name a single Gospel, much less say what's in it.

Learning how to be forgiven and how to pass that forgiveness on to others is an important part of our Christian life together. This practice of forgiving and being forgiven is nourished by other Christian practices such as baptism and Communion. Being baptized, whether as infants or as adults, initiates us into God's forgiveness and sets us on the lifelong journey of living into our baptism, of living into God's promises of forgiveness and new life. Sharing the Lord's Supper has a similarly formative effect. As we share, we recall the power of Christ's self-offering, remember the body of Christ as the community shares the Eucharistic meal, and anticipate the fullness of the messianic banquet at which God's reconciling work will be complete.

reflections

In addition, other practices such as prayer and healing can help us break apart cycles of self-deception, violence, and other forms of sin. Sometimes we can pray on behalf of others who aren't yet ready to ask or offer forgiveness in their own prayers. At other times, we pray for ourselves. In neither case is there a promise that prayer will work quickly. Sometimes forgiveness is a gift we recognize only after months, or perhaps years, of struggle. British author C. S. Lewis realized this and made the following note in his journal: "Last week, while at prayer, I suddenly discovered—or felt as if I did—that I had really forgiven someone I have been trying to forgive for over thirty years. Trying, and praying that I might."[7]

Sometimes forgiveness is a gift we recognize only after months, or perhaps years, of struggle.

UNLEARNING WHAT WE HAVE LEARNED

In order to embody forgiveness, we need to *unlearn* certain habits of thinking, feeling, and acting that divide and destroy communion, and we need to *learn* to see and live as forgiven and forgiving people. The words of Jesus call us to forgive without reservation or limit (Matthew 18:21-22). Different church traditions describe the practice of forgiveness in varying ways: confession, binding and loosing, penance, and reconciliation. Different traditions also see varying roles for clergy and laity in the practice. But there's agreement that among the essential features of this practice is the development of patterns of truthfulness in confronting sin and the seeking of reconciliation and new life.

reflections

We need to unlearn those ways of talking with one another that confuse, dominate, and control. In their place, we need to learn patterns of redemptive speech and silence that enable us to sustain community through the practice of forgiveness. Sometimes this may mean simply declining to speak rather than lashing out at someone. Being truthful doesn't mean saying everything we think, nor does it mean saying it in a judgmental way. Sometimes there's a redemptive silence to be offered through our physical presence when, perhaps, there's nothing much to be said.

Yet we also need to cultivate redemptive patterns of speech both in our discerning judgment and in the ways in which we offer or receive forgiveness. The Book of Ephesians instructs us to forgive one another as Christ forgives us. Significantly, this instruction is given at the close of a passage that urges us to "speak the truth" with one another (4:25–5:2). Trust is crucial if our practice is to edify rather than destroy.

HOW TO BE BLESSED

A central theme of the gospel is that God's grace and forgiveness are free gifts, undeserved and unmerited. God blesses us through Christ's redemption and calls us to develop the eyes to see and the ears to hear God's work in our own lives, in the lives of others, and in the world. God's blessing is thus discovered in our holy living, living that's shaped by the teachings of Christ.

In Matthew 5, Jesus speaks words of blessing to his followers in what we have come to call the Beatitudes. Last summer, our family stood at the site where tradition says Jesus spoke these words. When you stand on the top of the hill, the valley below forms a large, natural amphitheater that overlooks the Sea of Galilee. It appears to

reflections

be pristine, pastoral, serene. It feels like sacred space. Here, by the Sea of Galilee, there's a sense of peace; you can get a glimpse of the kingdom of heaven that Jesus was describing. And it's still there—as if lingering in the air, waiting for other expectant ears centuries later, waiting for others who still want to hear how to live lives that God would call "blessed."

As Jesus speaks, naming those who are blessed, his words surprise us. It's not the rich who are offered the kingdom of heaven. It's not those who are filled, satisfied, and accomplished. It's not those who are proud and strong. All the things we're taught to value so highly—achievement, strength, power, plenty—these are not what Jesus blesses here. Instead, he promises hope to the hopeless, comfort to the bereaved, satisfaction for the hungry and thirsty. He blesses the empty, those who are standing with hands open and outstretched, ready to receive. The Beatitudes are about what we cannot achieve, what we cannot accomplish, what we can only receive as the most startling of gifts. Only when we're emptied are we able to receive; only when we're hungry are we able to be filled; only when we're merciful will we find ourselves receiving mercy.

Learning to live as forgiven and forgiving people is both a gift and a lifelong task that can be communicated to the youngest child as well as to the oldest adult. Not one of us is finished learning the practice, and not one of us is without the ability to teach some aspect of it to others. We learn forgiveness in communities where people struggle to support and challenge one another, to trust one another, and to bear one another's burdens (Galatians 6:2). As we're embraced by communities of forgiveness, we come to discover the blessings found when, together, we seek to live the good life.

reflections

FAITHFUL FRIENDS: WATCHING OVER ONE ANOTHER IN LOVE

Use this space to record thoughts, reflections, insights, prayer concerns, or other matters that arise from your weekly conversations with faithful friends.

—4—

The Dance of Forgiveness

PSALM FOR PRAYING

Psalm 26:1-3

Vindicate me, O LORD,
>for I have walked in my integrity,
>and I have trusted in the LORD
>>without wavering.
Prove me, O LORD, and try me;
>test my heart and mind.
For your steadfast love is before my eyes,
>and I walk in faithfulness to you.

DAILY READINGS

DAY ONE
Ephesians 4:25-32 *(Speak the truth; God has forgiven us)*

These verses list negative behaviors that defeat communal life, followed by positive Christian alternatives

DAY TWO
Matthew 5:13-16, 21-24 *(The salt of the earth, light of the world; reconcile with your brother or sister)*

Transforming mission is the disciple's task Jesus exampled for this alternative community that embodies God's empire

DAY THREE
Matthew 6:9-15; Luke 11:2-4 *(The Lord's Prayer)*

Lord's prayer

DAY FOUR

Matthew 7:1-5 *(Speck in another's eye, log in your own)*

DAY FIVE

Romans 12:9-18 *(Bless those who persecute you)*

DAY SIX

Read the chapter on pages 42–47. You may take notes in the space provided at the bottom of each page.

H OW DO ORDINARY CHRISTIANS learn to practice forgiveness, to envision ways to build Christian communities
capable of embodying God's forgiveness? We suggest that
Christians can live into the patterns of forgiveness offered by
Christ if we begin to learn the steps of a beautiful—if sometimes
awkward—"dance of forgiveness."

CHRISTIAN CHARACTER IN CONTEXT

Here, briefly, are the six steps in the dance of forgiveness.

(1) *We become willing to speak truthfully and patiently about the cause
of the conflict.* This isn't easy, and there may not even be agreement
about what has happened. Therefore, we need not only truthfulness but also patience, the virtue that the ancient theologian
Tertullian called "the mother of mercy." When we try to be patient
and truthful, we can discern more clearly what's going on. James
1:19 reminds us, "Be quick to listen, slow to speak, slow to anger."

(2) *We acknowledge both the existence of anger and bitterness and the
desire to overcome them.* Whether these emotions are our own or
belong to the other party, it does no good to deny them. Anger
can be a sign of life, of passion. We should be more troubled by
those whose passion is hidden or, worse, extinguished. We can
learn to overcome and let go of anger and bitterness as we begin
to live differently through practices that transform hatred into
love. This is important, for otherwise anger can destroy others
and us. Ephesians 4:26 says, "Be angry but do not sin." We can't
let our anger get out of control and lead us into sin. As Frederick
Buechner puts it, "Of the Seven Deadly Sins, anger is possibly the

reflections

42

most fun. To lick your wounds, to smack your lips over grievances long past, to roll over your tongue the prospect of bitter confrontations still to come, to savor to the last toothsome morsel both the pain you are given and the pain you are giving back—in many ways it is a feast fit for a king. The chief drawback is that what you are wolfing down is yourself. The skeleton at the feast is you."[8]

(3) *We summon up a concern for the well-being of the other as a child of God.* Sometimes our partners in the dance of forgiveness are complete strangers. Other times they're persons intimately involved in our lives from whom we've become estranged. Either way, seeing them as children of God challenges our tendency to perceive them simply as enemies, rivals, or threats. They become potential friends in God. When someone asked Abraham Lincoln, after he had been elected president, what he planned to do about his enemies, it's said that he responded, "I am going to destroy them. I am going to make them my friends."[9]

(4) *We recognize our own complicity in the conflict, remember that we have been forgiven in the past, and take the step of repentance.* This doesn't mean ignoring differences between victims and victimizers. People need to be held accountable for their actions, and some people need to repent and ask forgiveness while those who have been victimized struggle to forgive. Even so, in all but the most extreme cases, we also need to recognize and resist our temptation to blame others while exonerating ourselves. All too often we see the specks in other people's eyes while not noticing the log in our own (Matthew 7:1-5). This is why it's important for us to remember our own forgiven-ness. Indeed, rather than "forgive and forget," a better description would be that we "forgive and are forgiven so we can remember well."

———————————————————————————

———————————————————————————

———————————————————————————

———————————————————————————

———————————————————————————

reflections

(5) *We make a commitment to struggle to change the conditions that perpetuate our conflicts.* Forgiveness doesn't merely refer backwards to the absolution of guilt; it also looks forward to the restoration of community. Forgiveness ought to usher in repentance and change; it ought to inspire prophetic protest wherever people's lives are being diminished or destroyed. Accountability plays an important role in forgiveness. Just because we're forgiven doesn't mean we won't be held accountable—and have to make reparations—for our actions. Forgiveness and justice are closely related.

> **Forgiveness doesn't merely refer backwards to the absolution of guilt; it also looks forward to the restoration of community.**

(6) *We confess our yearning for the possibility of reconciliation.* Sometimes a situation is so painful that reconciliation may seem impossible. At such times, prayer and struggle may be the only imaginable options. However, continuing to maintain reconciliation as the goal—even if this is "hoping against hope" for reconciliation in this life—is important as a way of reminding us of the ministry of reconciliation entrusted to us by God (2 Corinthians 5:16-21).

DANCING THE DANCE

As we learn to perform the dance of forgiveness in creative and innovative ways, we can more faithfully testify to Christ's reconciliation at work in our lives, our churches, and the world. We can do this as we learn—albeit slowly and often painfully—the habits and practices that shape a forgiven and forgiving people. This can

reflections

begin with a refusal to accept the loveless indifference that over time has created a chill in our relationships. Or it might begin with a commitment to abandoning the verbal and emotional abuse through which we diminish other people, or perhaps by refusing any longer to tolerate the ways in which we ourselves are diminished by such abuse. It might start with a steadfast commitment to pray for those who persecute us and others. Or we may decide to reestablish contact with someone from whom we became estranged years ago over some petty differences that nonetheless loomed large at the time.

After all, while we all pray that we'll never be faced with situations of extreme crisis that call for dramatic actions, we never know what might happen. Those of us who have, over time, cultivated holiness of heart, mind, and life will be better equipped to respond in ways that testify to God's gracious—and often surprising—offer of reconciliation. We need to tell the stories of exemplars of the faith, lifting up the ordinary and extraordinary ways in which they can stir our imaginations to offer gestures of powerful testimony.

These exemplars may include someone like Lloyd LeBlanc, a faithful Roman Catholic, whose story is recounted in the book *Dead Man Walking*. Upon discovering the body of his murdered son, LeBlanc immediately prayed the Lord's Prayer, repeating the words "Forgive us our trespasses as we forgive those who trespass against us." He acknowledges, "Forgiveness is never going to be easy. Each day it must be prayed for and struggled for and won."[10]

Such exemplars of faith also may include Kim Phuc, the Vietnamese woman who as a nine-year-old was photographed as she fled a Napalm attack, burns scarring her body. Her witness to forgiveness in various interviews has been read by many, including John Plummer, a pastor who was involved in the Napalm attack

reflections

and had been haunted by the memories of what he had done. Kim and John had a moving reconciliation at the Vietnam Veterans Memorial several years ago and have begun a new friendship in Christ.[11] Other exemplary persons can be found right in your own church or town.

COMMUNITIES OF FORGIVENESS

In addition to lifting up individual exemplars, we also need to celebrate exemplary communities that find ways to forgive and reconcile in their lives together. At a recent meeting in our denomination, the community was reminded how powerful the call to practices of forgiveness can be. Because the group had been struggling with internal divisions and bitterness among its churches, clergy, and lay members, it decided to structure its meeting around liturgies focused on forgiveness and reconciliation. The first night called the group to a confession of brokenness—a confession that included acknowledgment of how much easier it is to destroy trust than it is to rebuild it. During the service, each person was given a piece of glass to carry around for twenty-four hours. The next night was a service of forgiveness, and after a time of confession, various people collected the pieces of glass and took them to the altar. When all the glass had been collected and dumped in a large basket, a black cloth was removed from the altar to reveal a cross that had been made out of broken glass. The worshipers were reminded in image and

Christ's cross and resurrection transform human brokenness into communion.

reflections

words of the ways in which Christ's cross and resurrection transform human brokenness into communion. Everyone was invited to a time of prayer. Over the next day and a half, the group celebrated services of baptismal remembrance and Communion, reminding us all of the power of God's forgiveness to restore, reconcile, and make new. Toward the end of the meeting, a commissioning service sent people back to their communities and into the world as forgiven and forgiving people.

We ought to acknowledge, though, that such stories of dramatic exemplars might be not only inspiring but also paralyzing. What if we feel unable to respond as Lloyd LeBlanc or Kim Phuc did? What if our struggles with forgiveness arise not out of dramatic crises such as murder but emerge in the context of ongoing petty annoyances or a chilling apathy? What if the church in which we were raised has been more destructive than constructive in shaping our life?

Admittedly, one danger of focusing on extraordinary exemplars is that we can grow frustrated at our lack of progress. But here again, the language of practice and craft can be helpful. Just as one doesn't become an accomplished pianist overnight, neither should we expect ourselves to become accomplished at forgiveness so quickly. There's not just one way to display virtuosity either as a pianist or as an exemplar of forgiveness. We need to work graciously with ourselves and others to find the best way for us.

The dance of forgiveness is difficult to learn. Our ability to take the first halting steps is a testimony to the power of God's gracious, forgiving love. We *can* offer a witness that challenges hatred, vengeance, violence, and other forms of sin, a witness that shows people's lives can be changed by the grace of God in Jesus Christ. As we're invited to discover over and over again, forgiveness is an essential part of living the good life together.

reflections

FAITHFUL FRIENDS: WATCHING OVER ONE ANOTHER IN LOVE

Use this space to record thoughts, reflections, insights, prayer concerns, or other matters that arise from your weekly conversations with faithful friends.

—5—

Challenges to Forgiveness

PSALM FOR PRAYING

Psalm 25:6-7

Be mindful of your mercy, O LORD,
   and of your steadfast love,
for they have been from of old.
Do not remember the sins of my youth
   or my transgressions;
according to your steadfast love
   remember me,
for your goodness' sake, O LORD!

DAILY READINGS

DAY ONE
Ephesians 6:10-17 *(Be strong in the Lord)* 2097

all weapons are defensive except for the sword of the Spirit

DAY TWO
Luke 10:25-37 *(Love God with heart, soul, strength, and mind)*

The parable of the Good Samaritan

DAY THREE 2029
Ephesians 2:13-22 *(Christ has broken down the dividing wall)*

· One in Christ

DAY FOUR *n55*
Matthew 5:38-48 *(Turn the other cheek; go the second mile; love your enemies)* *Love your enemies*

DAY FIVE
Jonah 4:1-11 *(Jonah sits and sulks under a bush)* *1301*
Jonah's anger

DAY SIX
Read the chapter on pages 52–57. You may take notes in the space provided at the bottom of each page.

THE CONTRAST WAS STARK. Our family was attending a conference on forgiveness in Jerusalem, and very visible just to the south of the conference center at the checkpoint into Bethlehem was the new thirty-foot wall being built by the Israeli government to keep Palestinians confined to the West Bank. We were staying with Palestinian Christian friends in the little village of Beit Sahour, near Bethlehem, on the "other side" of the wall. In order to get to the conference each morning, our friends dropped us off on their side of the checkpoint—the closest to Jerusalem they were allowed to go. We waited in line at the checkpoint and then walked ten minutes up the hill to the conference center after passing the thirty-foot wall. What did the conference on forgiveness have to do with the divisions that were so visibly facing us, including the fact that our friends weren't allowed to cross the checkpoint and therefore couldn't attend the conference with us?

The Israeli government said building the wall was for "security," but the more we heard this line of reasoning, the more we wondered, *Don't we usually build walls around us because of insecurity?* The wall seemed a desperate attempt to end violence. Yet its overwhelming presence took us in our minds to Berlin, to the townships of South Africa, and to other failed attempts to solve conflict by division.

We found ourselves returning to the checkpoint and the wall each day, noticing how they were marking our perceptions as deeply as they had marked the landscape around us. What must it be like for the people who confront security checkpoints every day? Is it possible to overcome the wall's ominous presence and symbolic power? How can the people prevent bitterness and

reflections

despair—even rage and the desire for revenge—from overwhelming them?

We asked a Palestinian friend those questions at dinner on our last night in the West Bank. Our friend, a theology student at Bethlehem Bible College, acknowledged how bleak the situation there felt. We talked about how in the late 1980s in South Africa, each side had predicted that more than three million people would be killed before their side was victorious. But shortly thereafter, Nelson Mandela was released, apartheid ended, and a peaceful transition to democracy occurred rather than the war that had been predicted. "This," he said, "is what we need most." He reached for a pen, and on his napkin he wrote out four letters in bold print and underlined them: H-O-P-E.

CHRISTIAN CHARACTER IN CONTEXT

If we build walls, we build animosity, mistrust, and despair. If we build bridges, we connect people and invite them into relationship with one another.

In Luke 10, a teacher of the law stands up to test Jesus with the question "What must I do to inherit eternal life?" Jesus refers him to the Hebrew Scriptures, in which the man was well-versed. The lawyer answers his own question by quoting verses from Deuteronomy and Leviticus: to love God with all your heart, soul, strength, and mind, and to love your neighbor as yourself. Jesus affirms his answer, saying, "Do this, and you will live." But this doesn't satisfy the lawyer. Wanting to justify himself, the lawyer adds another question: "And who is my neighbor?" Rather than answering that question, Jesus tells the parable of the good

reflections

53

Samaritan, a story that flips the question on its head by asking, "To whom am I called to be a neighbor?"

On our trip to the Middle East, our family traveled from Jerusalem to Jericho down the same road traveled by the good Samaritan. It's still a deserted place marked by only by a few nomads and kibbutzes. Lying beaten by the side of that road, the man described in the story must have thought he was more than just "half dead." He had had two chances to be rescued, and both had passed him by. We're not told why the priest and Levite did not stop. Was it fear? Was it concern about purity laws and proper conduct? Who knows? For whatever reason, the religious authorities showed no mercy to the one who was in need.

But the Samaritan, whose people were hated by the Jews, had something the two religious leaders didn't: He had eyes to see, a heart filled with pity, and hands and feet that moved him to take a risk, bind up the wounds of a total stranger, and carry him to a place where he could receive care. He did all this not knowing if the robbers were still lurking behind some large rock or were just around the bend, ready to return and attack again. It was the Samaritan who took the risk to show mercy, in light of which Jesus says, "Go and do likewise" (Luke 10:37).

BREAKING DOWN BOUNDARIES

The Samaritan's care for his "enemy" broke down boundaries and reframed relationships. Yet communities can't exist without some boundaries, particularly if hostility and a lack of repentance are present. Those who refuse to repent may risk excluding themselves from forgiveness, as Matthew 18:15-20 shows. Such exclusion,

reflections

however, ought to be seen as only temporary and always in the context of the hope that they will return to the fellowship. We aren't allowed to demonize them; rather, we're called to love them (Matthew 5:44). Just as Jesus reached out to Gentiles and tax collectors, seeking to bring them back into the fold of God's grace, so also are we called to continue to reach out to—and love—our enemies. We can't allow even legitimate boundaries to become impenetrable barriers.

> **We can't allow even legitimate boundaries to become impenetrable barriers.**

It's challenging to risk loving enemies, those people who mean us harm and aren't repentant. This task is difficult but not impossible, whether for Palestinians and Jews, for members of denominations who end up on opposite sides of divisive issues, or for those of us trying to relate to very difficult people within our own families. Sometimes we wonder if the reason Jesus tells us to love both our enemies *and* our neighbors is because sometimes they end up being the same people. It's not easy to make room in our lives for strangers, for those in need, and even for enemies, but in order to find life in Christ, we must try. For Jesus says, "Do this, and you will live" (Luke 10:28).

LOVING OUR ENEMIES

Loving our enemies is easier to do in the abstract than in flesh and blood. This is as true of those enemies who explicitly intend us harm as it is of those with whom we fundamentally disagree.

reflections

In Wendell Berry's novel *Jayber Crow,* the title character is a barber in a small Kentucky town. Jayber interacts with a variety of people as they come to his barbershop, and he struggles particularly with Troy Chatham, a greedy farmer whom Jayber thinks is destroying the land in their county. To make matters worse, Troy has also married a woman whom Jayber had secretly admired for several years.

One Saturday evening in the barbershop, while Troy is waiting his turn in the chair, he launches into a diatribe against war protesters. Jayber says,

> It was hard to do, but I quit cutting hair and looked at Troy. I said, "Love your enemies, bless them that curse you, do good to them that hate you."
>
> Troy jerked his head up and widened his eyes at me. "Where did you get that crap?"
>
> I said, "Jesus Christ."
>
> And Troy said, "Oh."
>
> It would have been a great moment in the history of Christianity, except that I did not love Troy.[12]

As difficult as it may be, it's only in those flesh-and-blood relationships—in trying to love the Troys of our lives—that we learn what it really means to love our enemies. Such schooling is necessary if we are to make larger-scale commitments to love our enemies. Churches need to become schools for learning love—whether of strangers, friends, or enemies—so that, as Jayber might have said, we might be better prepared to produce great and small moments in the history of Christianity.

reflections

THE COST OF DISCIPLESHIP

Forgiveness shouldn't be used as a means of evading responsibility or of seeking cheap grace. As Dietrich Bonhoeffer described it in *The Cost of Discipleship,* "Cheap grace is the preaching of forgiveness without requiring repentance, baptism without church discipline, Communion without confession, absolution without personal confession. Cheap grace is grace without discipleship, grace without the cross, grace without Jesus Christ, living and incarnate."[13] The practice of forgiveness involves hard work, including our resistance to those forces in our lives and our world that diminish or destroy ourselves, others, and the fragile communities in which we live.

Forgiveness shouldn't be used as a means of evading responsibility or of seeking cheap grace.

All this suggests that we need the support and discerning help of others as we learn how to forgive and be forgiven. When we encourage one another through the challenges of forgiveness, we participate in Christ's work of breaking down the dividing walls of hostility. We learn together, one day at a time, that as we forgive others and as we allow ourselves to be forgiven, we build bridges that lead us to a place where we truly do live the good life.

reflections

FAITHFUL FRIENDS: WATCHING OVER ONE ANOTHER IN LOVE

Use this space to record thoughts, reflections, insights, prayer concerns, or other matters that arise from your weekly conversations with faithful friends.

—6—

Planning the Next Steps Together

Psalm 139:23-24

Search me, O God, and know my heart;
    test me and know my thoughts.
See if there is any wicked way in me,
    and lead me in the way everlasting.

FOR THE PAST FEW WEEKS you have experienced the "Come and See" portion of this study, exploring aspects of the Christian character trait of forgiveness. You have learned about and reflected upon "The Heart of Christian Living," "Crafting Communities of Forgiveness," "The Dance of Forgiveness," and "Challenges to Forgiveness." You have experienced psalms for praying and lectio divina to engage Scripture in a prayerful way. You have communicated regularly as faithful friends with another person in the group. You have learned all this in the company of other Christians who also seek God's "good life."

In the space provided below, take some time now to write about particular learnings from the previous sessions that have been meaningful or significant to you.

The time has come to move from understanding forgiveness to developing practices of forgiveness. It is time to "Go and Do" forgiveness in your group.

At your next session, you and your group will plan together how to "try out" what you have learned about the Christian character trait of forgiveness. Then, for the weeks to follow, you will put your plan into action, both as individuals and as a group.

Your group planning session will be most effective if each member, in preparation for the session, takes a few minutes to brainstorm ways in which the group can begin to practice forgiveness over the next six weeks during the "Go and Do" portion of the study.

On the pages that follow, you will see several boxes, each of which contains an idea prompt. These idea prompts are designed to help you imagine ways in which you and your group could put into practice what you have learned about forgiveness. Allow your mind to explore every possible avenue for embodying this notion of forgiveness in your life as a Christian. Resist the tendency to edit your ideas; instead, record all of them in the spaces provided. Be ready to share them with the group when you meet.

As you consider and record your ideas, keep in mind that ideas are only a part of Christian character. Christianity comes alive only when, inspired by ideas, we move into the world, practicing and embodying our faith. That's when we truly become the body of Christ and begin—haltingly at first but then with confidence and faith—living the good life together.

Lectio divina Scripture passages

Behavioral changes to make

Ministry events to consider

Mission work to conceive and implement

Speakers to invite

Field trips, retreats, pilgrimages to take

Books to read, movies to see

Other ideas

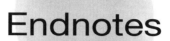

Endnotes

1. Adapted by permission from *50 Ways to Pray: Practices From Many Traditions and Times,* by Teresa A. Blythe (Abingdon Press, 2006); pages 45–47.
2. From *Love and Justice: Selections From the Shorter Writings of Reinhold Niebuhr,* by Reinhold Niebuhr (Westminster/John Knox Press, 1957); page 269.
3. From *Living in the Forgiveness of God,* by James R. Bjorge (Augsburg Fortress, 1990); pages 9–10.
4. The sculpture is called *Reconciliation,* by Margaret Adams Parker.
5. From *Lament for a Son,* by Nicholas Wolterstorff (Wm. B. Eerdmans Publishing Company, 1987); page 86.
6. From *Beloved,* by Toni Morrison (Plume, 1987); pages 172–73.

7. From *Letters to Malcolm: Chiefly on Prayer*, by C. S. Lewis (Harcourt Brace, 1964); page 106.

8. From *Wishful Thinking: A Theological ABC*, by Frederick Buechner (Harper & Row Publishers, 1973); page 2.

9. This is an unverified quotation often attributed to Abraham Lincoln. See http://www.bartleby.com/73/689.html.

10. From *Dead Man Walking: An Eyewitness Account of the Death Penalty in the United States*, by Sister Helen Prejean (Vintage Books, 1993); pages 244–45.

11. See "A Picture of Forgiveness," in *The Christian Century*, February 19, 1997. The article can be found online at http://www.findarticles.com/p/articles/mi_m1058/is_n6_v114/ai_19174188.

12. From *Jayber Crow: A Novel*, by Wendell Berry (Counterpoint, 2000); page 287.

13. From *The Cost of Discipleship*, by Dietrich Bonhoeffer (SCM Press Ltd, 1959); page 47.

ACKNOWLEDGMENTS

Living the Good Life Together: A Study of Christian Character in Community is the result of a very good idea. The idea was that the church needed help in teaching God's people to cultivate patterns or practices of holy living—in other words, to learn to live a good life as defined by Scripture and exemplified by Jesus. This idea became the subject of a very fruitful conversation, thanks especially to the participation of Timothy W. Whitaker, Resident Bishop of the Florida Annual Conference of The United Methodist Church; L. Gregory Jones, Dean and Professor of Theology at Duke University Divinity School; and Paul W. Chilcote, Professor of Historical Theology and Wesleyan Studies at Asbury Theological Seminary in Florida. Their commitment to the idea and their contributions to the development process provided the vision and the impetus for this unique resource.